THE INTERVIEWER'S POCKETBOOK

3rd Edition

By Sean McManus & John Townsend

Drawings by Phil Hailstone

Published by:
Management Pocketbooks Ltd
Laurel House, Station Approach, Alresford, Hants SO24 9JH, U.K.
Tel: +44 (0)1962 735573 Fax: +44 (0)1962 733637
Email: sales@pocketbook.co.uk
Website: www.pocketbook.co.uk

First edition 1987, Second edition 1999 © John Townsend
ISBN 978 1 870471 75 6

This edition published 2014
©   Sean McManus & John Townsend
ISBN 978 1 906610 78 4
E-book ISBN 978 1 908284 42 6

British Library Cataloguing-in-Publication Data – A catalogue record for this book is available from the British Library.

Design, typesetting and graphics by **efex ltd**.   Printed in U.K.

CONTENTS

4

Understanding Interviews

ABOUT THIS BOOK

Conducting a good recruitment interview is hard, much harder than people expect, and the process often fails. A survey of hiring managers conducted by Harris Interactive on behalf of Careerbuilder found that 62% of UK hiring managers had hired someone who turned out to be a bad fit for the job, or unable to do it*. 27% of UK companies said that a bad hire cost them more than £50,000.

The popular belief that you can 'just tell' whether someone will be good at a job has been proven wrong in practice, again and again. In order to hire the right people into your organisation, your interview process must be reliable, consistent and fair.

This book will help you to develop your skills in asking questions, listening, using body language, preparing interviews and conducting them. As a result, it will help you to make sure you're recruiting the very best people into your organisation.

* More Than Half of Companies in the Top Ten World Economies Have Been Affected By a Bad Hire, According to CareerBuilder Survey, 8 May 2013

WHY GOOD INTERVIEWS MATTER

Why is good selection interviewing important?

Success	Your personal success depends on the quality of the people you hire.
Cost	Selection mistakes can cost thousands.
Growth	Your organisation's growth depends on your ability to attract and keep good people.
Reputation	The selection interview is a dialogue with the labour market. The way you conduct interviews will be fed back to the market and can create (or destroy) a reputation.
Development	If you select mediocre people you can't develop them into future leaders.

THE STAKES ARE HIGH

For the employer, a wrong hiring decision can be expensive. It often leads to:
- Unplanned training costs
- Unexpectedly low productivity
- Missed sales and growth opportunities

Ultimately, the whole recruitment process must be repeated, setting the company back months. Those interviewing must take more time out of their day-to-day work for further interviews, and advertising and agency fees must be paid again. Apart from the visible costs, a bad hiring decision can also disrupt the team and sap morale.

For the interviewee, there's a lot at stake too. They might leave a job where they're happy so they can join your company. They might even relocate. If they don't match your job requirements well, they'll struggle to perform the job and will be unhappy. Ultimately, they are likely to leave the company and will have to find a suitable job elsewhere.

THE INTERVIEW CHALLENGE

The interview is an artificial conversation, and the performance of the candidate is often skewed by that. It might be hard to rely on the answers you get.

- Candidates are likely to be nervous and experiencing a type of stress very different to the strains of the job you're hiring for

- Candidates will present their best side to you

- Candidates might have anticipated some of your questions and prepared 'right' answers

- What people say they do and what they actually do might be very different

- Candidates might exaggerate their talents, or lack the self-awareness to recognise their limitations

THE INTERVIEW CHALLENGE

For many interviewers, the interview is a mysterious process.

- Few interviewers have been trained to carry out interviews. They draw upon the interviews they've experienced, so bad practice passes from generation to generation of manager

- Because they don't have enough training, interviewers often rely on gut instinct or chemistry. But hiring someone you like doesn't mean they can do the job. Because of the artificial nature of the interview, it doesn't even guarantee they'll get on with colleagues

- Outside of human resources departments, managers conduct selection interviews infrequently. They don't get enough practice with real candidates to perfect their interviewing skills

WHAT MAKES A SUCCESSFUL INTERVIEW?

A successful interview cycle is one where:

- The interviewer is able to **assess** the ability of candidates to do the job they have applied for
- The interviewer gathers **evidence** of candidates' abilities that will support a hiring decision after the interviews conclude
- The interviewer can clearly **differentiate** between the abilities of the different interviewees

- Candidates are given a good opportunity to present their experience and skills
- Candidates and the interviewer are satisfied that the process was **fair** and candidates were judged solely on their ability to perform the job in question

COMMON INTERVIEW MISTAKES

There are some mistakes that interviewers often make:

- **Poor preparation**: an interviewer must enter the interview with a good understanding of the role they are hiring for, and the competencies required to perform it

- **Asking weak questions**: if candidates can guess the answer the interviewer wants, or if all candidates are likely to give the same answer, the question won't help to tell candidates apart

- **Ceding control**: letting candidates steer conversation into areas where they are more comfortable, rather than sticking to what the interviewer needs to know

- **Not getting the information required**: a good interviewer will prompt the candidate to reveal the information they need, without leading them into falsifying it

COMMON INTERVIEW MISTAKES

- **Halo and horns effects**: allowing particularly good or bad performance in one area to shape the interviewer's perception of other areas, or the candidate as a whole

- **Straying into unethical areas**: if the interviewer asks about family background, health, age or religion it creates the impression that candidates are being assessed differently on those grounds, which would be illegal

- **Straying into chitchat**: a good interviewer will make candidates feel relaxed, but if conversation strays into shared interests, the interview can lose focus. Candidates might also have the impression they are being judged on their interests, rather than their ability to perform the job, which would be unfair and unethical

WHICH SKILLS DO YOU NEED?

Interviewers can avoid these mistakes and help to minimise the risk that interviews present to the organisation and the candidate by acquiring good interviewing skills.

These include:

- **Questioning skills**: Knowing the right questions to ask helps to solicit the answers you need. Not all questions can be prepared in advance, so you need to know how to probe for more information when necessary

- **Listening skills**: Actively listening to candidates so that you can steer the interview based on what they tell you, and what they haven't told you yet

- **Body language skills**: Using your own body language to build rapport, and watching candidates' body language to identify further questioning opportunities

- **Preparation skills**: Entering the interview room with a good understanding of the information required, and the questions you'll ask to get it

Although our focus here is on the selection interview, many of these skills are also valuable in other managerial meetings, including appraisals, discipline interviews, fact-finding meetings and line management meetings.

QUESTIONING TECHNIQUES

QUESTIONING TECHNIQUES

A WORD OF WARNING

The great majority of interviewers ask terrible questions. Asking good questions is not a natural human talent. Our tendency in any kind of interview is to talk too much, to lead the interviewee towards our own way of thinking and to overload him or her with multiple questions.

The result is an interview where the limited amount of information obtained is of poor quality.

Then we wonder why decisions taken on the basis of the information obtained turn out to be wrong!

TYPES OF QUESTIONS

There are lots of different kinds of questions you can ask in an interview. A typical interview will draw on several of them, perhaps all of them.

Knowing the different types of question can help you to ask the right one at the right time.

The main question types are:
- Open
- Closed
- Evidence
- Hypothetical
- Probing
- Blockbusting
- Framing
- Challenge
- Reflective

OPEN QUESTIONS

An open question is one to which there are many possible answers.

Examples
- Why did you launch the product in the summer?
- How did you win support from management for that idea?
- What were the biggest challenges you faced on that project?
- How did you allocate your marketing budget?
- How did you choose what to stock?

When to ask
To explore the candidate's experience and thinking

CLOSED QUESTIONS

A closed question is one to which there is only one right answer.

Examples

- When did you join your last company?
- Which computer system were you using at that time?
- Who was your manager then?
- How many people were in your team?
- What was your job title after the promotion?

When to ask
To fill in details

EVIDENCE QUESTIONS

The **best** way to find out whether a candidate has the skills and experience you need, is to ask them for examples of when they have used them in a previous job, or outside work.

Examples

- Tell me about a time when you dealt with an angry customer
- Describe an occasion when you had conflicting deadlines
- Give me an example of when you negotiated with a supplier

When to ask

- To prompt the candidate to tell you about their relevant experience
- All candidates should be asked the same evidence questions

HYPOTHETICAL QUESTIONS

Hypothetical questions are open questions that ask for information in an **imaginary** scenario.

Examples
- What would you do if a customer threatened to begin legal proceedings?
- If an employee you were managing was behaving dangerously, what would you do?
- Let's imagine I'm a supermarket purchasing manager. Show me how you would pitch a new confectionery item on your initial sales call

When to ask
- When a candidate doesn't have relevant experience in a particular area, to check whether they know the right approach
- To probe for more detail on the candidate's thinking and strategies
- Occasionally, role playing can enable you to see their relevant skills first-hand

Remember that what people say they would do and what they actually do can be very different.

PROBING QUESTIONS

Probing questions are closed questions seeking **specific information** you need.

Examples
- What is your current job title?
- What's the turnover of ABC Ltd?
- How many direct reports do you have?
- Are you responsible for making purchasing decisions?

When to ask
- When you want to probe for facts or details
- When the interviewee is rambling or talking too much
- After an evidence or hypothetical question, to get more specific information on the candidate's answer

PROBING QUESTIONS

GATHERING COMPLETE INFORMATION

As candidates answer your evidence questions, they will tell you about achievements and episodes from their work and their outside interests. Make sure you get a complete picture by digging into the details with your probing questions.

You need to know:

What happened? What was the final outcome?

Why did this happen? What was the cause, and the goal?

When did this happen? More recent examples suggest candidates are using the skills more often.

Who was involved in the project? Take particular care when candidates use the word 'we'. Make sure you understand their particular contribution.

Where did this happen? Was this in their current company, or in an extra-curricular group?

How did they go about tackling the challenge? 

BLOCKBUSTING QUESTIONS

Blockbusting questions are closed questions which ask for more **precision** in the information provided by the interviewee.

Examples	**When to ask**
Which (noun) exactly?	When you need more precise details.
How did you (verb) exactly?	When you need more precise details.
All? Never? Everyone?	After broad statements using words such as *all, never, none, everyone, always, nobody*.
Compared to what? 	After vague comparisons using words such as *better, best, faster, increased, improved, less, more*.

24

FRAMING QUESTIONS

A framing question is a type of open question that asks for information to give you more context about why something was done, or why it matters.

Examples

What was the objective of that project? **(Outcome Frame)**

What were the constraints on your decision at that time? **(Backtrack Frame)**

Help me to see how this contributed to your sales targets. **(Relevance Frame)**

When to ask

To clarify the overarching goal of a project or team, so you can confirm the candidate's decisions and actions were consistent with it.

To provide context for the actions taken and decisions made.

To get the interview back on track if you can't see why a point was brought up, but you want to give the interviewee the benefit of the doubt.

CHALLENGE QUESTIONS

This type of open question challenges the interviewee to provide **back-up information**.

What would you accept as evidence you've improved customer service?
(Evidence challenge)

What would argue against that approach?
(Devil's advocate challenge)

REFLECTIVE QUESTIONS

Reflective questions **reflect back** to the interviewee what you think they mean or said.

Examples
- If I understand you correctly, you were covering someone else's job at the same time?
- In other words, you decided to escalate the issue to your manager?
- So, that's why you ended up leaving the position? 

When to ask
- To clarify or confirm your understanding of the situation
- To help the interviewee to articulate what they mean
- To show the interviewee you are listening
- To onoourago tho intorviowoo to continuo rolating tho story

ADDITIONAL TECHNIQUES

You can smooth out the cold, analytical questioning process with two additional techniques:

Factual linking
Building links or bridges between the information being provided and the areas of concern to the interviewer.

Example
You mentioned just now that one of your objectives is to create a team spirit within the department. I'd be interested in hearing about the kind of measurement you'll use to judge how successful you've been. **(Evidence challenge)**

Empathetic linking
Showing interest and concern about the information being provided.

Example
It sounds like this was a tough time in your division. Tell me, how specifically did you deal with the communication problem? **(Verb blockbuster)**

KEEPING THE INTERVIEWEE ON TRACK

It's OK to **sensitively interrupt** the candidate if they stray off-track.

In particular, look out for candidates who answer evidence questions as if they were hypothetical questions.

Example

Interviewer  Can you give me an example of when you had to deal with a dissatisfied customer?

Interviewee Usually, with situations like this I start by calling the customer to find out what their concern is.

Interviewer That makes sense, but I'd really like to hear about a specific occasion when you had this challenge. What was the most recent cause of dissatisfaction?

QUESTIONING TECHNIQUES

SILENCE

Silence can be a useful questioning technique. Resist the urge to fill it.

Examples	**When to use**
Up to 5 seconds' silence	To allow interviewee to collect thoughts; courtesy.
5-15 seconds' silence	To encourage interviewees to share information they probably want to keep to themselves.

QUESTIONS TO AVOID

LEADING QUESTIONS

There are several types of question you should avoid, starting with leading questions. These are questions that indicate the desired response.

Examples
- Would you say you're a people person?
- All our bonuses here are based on customer satisfaction. What do you think is the most important aspect of team performance?
- I see you were promoted after two years in your previous role. You must have done a good job, then?

The only way an interviewee can provide any high quality information is by disagreeing with you. That is unlikely to happen in an interview.

Be careful: nobody sets out to ask a leading question, but it's easy to lapse into one.

PSYCHOLOGY QUESTIONS

Some interviewers have used questions like the following to try to understand the candidate's personality better:

- If you were an animal, what kind of animal would you be?
- Tell me about the last book you read
- What would you do if you were prime minister for a day?

PSYCHOLOGY QUESTIONS

Psychology questions should never be used, because:

- The answers don't tell you anything reliable. They're subject to the interviewer's interpretation
- The answers don't reveal how well the candidate can do the job
- The questions result in managers hiring people like them, rather than people who are the best fit for the role under discussion
- These questions can create an impression that the selection process is unfair and based on opinions and personalities, rather than focused on finding the best person for the job
- Many candidates will not want to work for a company that bases important decisions on trivia

DISCRIMINATORY QUESTIONS

It's **unethical** and **illegal** to discriminate against candidates for their:

- Gender
- Race
- Disability
- Sexual orientation
- Religion
- Age

If a candidate makes a complaint on any of these grounds, the onus is on you to justify your hiring decision.

To avoid misunderstandings, **do not ask** questions about age, family background, childcare arrangements, health, or groups or campaigns somebody may belong to (which could reveal information on **sexuality** or religion). Limit your questions to the skills, behaviours and experience required to carry out the functions of the job.

DISCRIMINATORY QUESTIONS

In certain **rare** cases where the role **demands** particular physical capabilities, there is a legal exception and it can be acceptable to ask a health-related question.

For example, if the role requires heavy lifting, you can ask whether somebody is able to do heavy lifting (with reasonable adjustments if necessary). Reasonable adjustments include things like changes to equipment, procedures and the workplace layout. You are not allowed to discriminate against candidates because they need reasonable adjustments to be made.

The nature of any reasonable adjustments should be discussed after a job offer has been made, to avoid accusations of discrimination in the recruitment process. If the candidate brings them up, tell them they will be discussed with the successful candidate after the job offer has been made.

SELF-APPRAISAL QUESTIONS

Don't ask candidates to appraise themselves, with questions like:
- What would you say are your weaknesses?
- What are your greatest strengths? 

Candidates will tell you their strengths are exactly those required by the job, and are unlikely to be candid about real weaknesses. They might 'reveal' weaknesses that include *working too hard* and *being a bit too much of a perfectionist, sometimes*.

There are many books that include suggested answers to questions like these, and some of your candidates have probably read them.

BRAINTEASER QUESTIONS

Brainteaser questions like these have been used by Microsoft, Google and other technology companies:

- How many piano tuners are there in the world?
- How many times a day do a clock's hands overlap?
- How many golf balls can fit in a school bus?

In theory, brainteasers challenge a candidate's creativity and give the interviewer the opportunity to listen in on the candidate's thinking process. In practice, the reasoning required bears no relation to the skills of the job.

BRAINTEASER QUESTIONS

You can't guarantee a spontaneous response, either. Candidates can find answers to questions like these online and rehearse them in advance, putting on a good show of spontaneity in the interview.

Google has abandoned this style of questioning. *'We found that brainteasers are a complete waste of time'*, said Laszlo Bock, senior vice president of people operations at Google. *'They don't predict anything'.**

Unless you're hiring guests for a quiz show, don't ask questions like these!

*In Head-Hunting, Big Data May Not Be Such a Big Deal, New York Times; 19 June 2013

MULTIPLE QUESTIONS

A multiple question is a string of several questions:

> Give me an example of a time when you disagreed with a manager. What did you disagree about? I'd be interested to know how you resolved the disagreement. Were you both satisfied with the outcome? Tell me what you'd do differently next time.

Never ask a multiple question. The interviewee will only answer the last question or the easiest one. So, why not ask the last one or the easiest one instead?

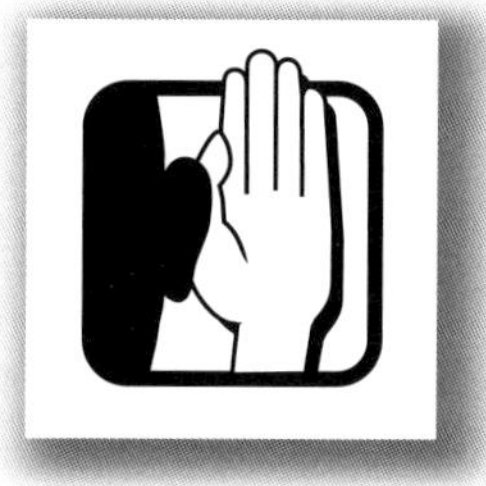

LISTENING TECHNIQUES

GOOD LISTENING SKILLS

There's not much point asking the perfect question
if you don't listen to the answer.

Good listening skills are important because:
- They enable you to capture the
  information that will help you make a
  hiring decision
- They help you to build rapport with
  interviewees, so they are more
  open and honest in their answers
- They help you to shape your
  questions, so you can ensure you
  don't miss out anything important

LISTENING TECHNIQUES

THE 30/70 RULE

Most of the time during an interview, you will be listening, not speaking.

As a guide, the candidate usually speaks for 70% of the time and you speak for only 30% of the time. After all, who's the one being interviewed?

LISTENING BARRIERS

Here are nine behaviours that prevent us from becoming better listeners:

1. Scoring points
(Relating everything you hear to your own experience)
- Saying, *'Oh, that's nothing, you should have seen what happened to me last week!'*
- Thinking, *My colleagues are so much more intelligent than that!*

2. Mind reading
(Predicting what the interviewee is really thinking)
- Saying to yourself, *'I bet that's not the real reason he left XYZ!'*

3. Rehearsing
(Practising your next lines in your head)
- Preparing your next 'clever' question and missing the current answer

LISTENING BARRIERS

4. Cherry picking
(Listening for a key piece of information – then switching off)
- Checking that an interviewee has business-to-business sales experience and then not listening to the details

5. Daydreaming
(Letting your mind wander and losing focus on the interview)
- You can think four to six times faster than people can talk. The temptation is to use the 'spare' time to daydream

6. Labelling
(Putting an interviewee into a category before hearing all the evidence)
- Quickly dubbing an interviewee as a 'typical' accountant/ salesperson, etc
- Not listening to an interviewee who you've decided is a rambler, etc

LISTENING BARRIERS

7. Counselling
(Being unable to resist interrupting and giving advice)
- Saying, *'Why don't you try ...'* or *'In my experience, the best ...'*

8. Duelling
(Countering an interviewee's statements by bragging about your team or company)
- Saying, *'Well, at least this department is never over budget!'*
- Saying, *'You won't find people in this company acting like that!'*

9. Side-stepping sentiment
(Countering expressions of emotion with jokes or hollow clichés)
- Saying, *'Well, it's not the end of the world, is it?'*
- Saying, *'Oh well, never mind, could have been worse!'*

YOU CAN'T MULTITASK LISTENING

To listen to an interviewee effectively, you need to focus your attention on them completely. Eliminate distractions.

You can't read email notifications or text messages and listen properly at the same time. It's probably best to leave computers, phones and other devices outside the interview room.

TAKING NOTES

Should you take notes during an interview?

Yes, because:
- It enables you to capture everything. If you rely on your memory, you'll only remember the highlights and lowlights of what was said
- It enables you to stay neutral. Capture the information, and you can make a decision using it later
- It enables you to prove the selection process was fair, by preserving a record of the evidence on which your hiring decision was based

Note-taking shows interviewees you are taking their information-giving seriously.

Try to maintain sensitive eye contact when you're not writing, to reassure candidates.

HEARING CLEARLY

It might seem obvious, but you can't interview someone if you can't hear them clearly. Noisy rooms can make it tiring to conduct an interview, and difficult to properly listen.

Find a quiet space, ideally a room where you can close the door, to conduct the interview.

If you're carrying out an initial interview by phone or video and can't hear properly, see if you can try again for a better connection. It's hard to build rapport if you're struggling to understand.

PARALINGUISTICS

Paralinguistics refer to **the way** that something is said. Paralinguistics can affect the meaning of a candidate's answer, and your interpretation of it, as much as the words chosen. You should be aware of several different aspects of paralinguistics outlined below.

TYPE	INTERPRETATION
Timing	Short answers might indicate shyness, but could also depend on the questions you ask. Closed questions will trigger short replies.
Tone/ inflection	Tone conveys emotions being felt by the interviewee and can help you identify the image he or she wants to project.
Speech errors	Speech errors can indicate fatigue, stress, or anxiety. Hesitations like *er* and *um* are just used to buy thinking time.
Accent	Tells you where the interviewee comes from.

PARALINGUISTICS

TYPE	INTERPRETATION
Choice of words	Gives colour to speech and indicates level of education, attitude towards subject matter and degree of formality perceived.
Verbal tics	Verbal mannerisms could indicate poor vocabulary, laziness, fashion influence, messy thinking or just plain habit.
Emphasis	Tonic accents on syllables and words signpost the real meaning (eg *I know how **you** feel about the situation*). Listen to make sure you catch the right emphasis.

INTERPRETING PARALINGUISTICS

It's important to be aware of paralinguistics, but take care with how you interpret them.

DO NOT:

✗ **Mind read**. If the tone is at odds with the words being spoken, probe deeper to find out why. Don't assume you know why an interviewee appears emotional

✗ **Get distracted**. It's easy to be impressed when somebody speaks articulately, but unless that is a required behaviour for the job (for example, for a press spokesperson), it's not relevant. The experience and skills matter, not how well the interviewee can tell you about them

✗ **Judge accents and tics**. Where a candidate comes from is also not relevant, and tics only matter if the role requires perfect speech. Again, how well someone can tell you about their skills and experience is rarely relevant

Understanding Body Language

USING BODY LANGUAGE

A lot of communication happens non-verbally, for example through facial expressions and body posture.

An understanding of body language is useful to you in two ways:

- You can use your own body language to build rapport and encourage the interviewee to open up

- You can observe the interviewee's body language to identify questions that might be uncomfortable for them, so that you can ask appropriate follow-up questions to find out why

TYPES OF BODY LANGUAGE

P ostures & gestures — How does the interviewee use hand gestures? What about his/ her sitting position?

E ye contact — How often do your eyes meet? For how long?

O rientation — How does the interviewee position himself/ herself to you?

P roximity — How close do you sit to the interviewee?

L ooks/ appearance — Are looks/ appearance important for the job?

E xpressions of emotion — Can you trust facial expressions as signposts to emotion?

We will look at each of these in turn.

POSTURES & GESTURES: HANDS

STEEPLING
- Self-confidence (intellectual arrogance)

NOSE TOUCH
- Doubt or deceit

MOUTH BLOCK
- Resisting speech

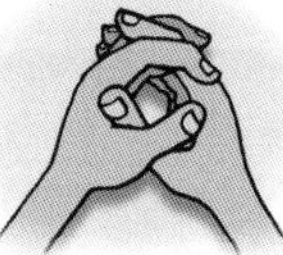

HAND CLASP
- Anxious, controlled

'L' CHIN REST
- Critical evaluation

EYE RUB
- Doubt or deceit

POSTURES & GESTURES: SITTING

ARMS UP

- Reserved, defensive

ARM/ LEG CROSS

- Closed, unconvinced, unengaged

LEAN FORWARD

- Ready!

POSTURES & GESTURES: SITTING

LEAN BACK

- Confident superiority

LINT-PICKING

- Disapproval

UNDERSTANDING BODY LANGUAGE

EYE CONTACT

Studies by Michael Argyle show that during the average European conversation:

- The listener looks at the speaker for 75% of the time
- The speaker looks at the listener for 40% of the time
- Both look each other in the eye for 30% of the time
- The length of each mutual glance is only 1.5 seconds

Eye contact is important for building rapport, so if you're taking notes, look up from time to time, especially when you're asking a question.

The important thing is to use eye contact in a way that feels comfortable.

ORIENTATION

As the host of the interview, and the person responsible for the furniture in the room, you have most control over the interviewee's orientation to you.

Avoid sitting behind a desk, because that creates a barrier that can make it hard to strike up rapport, and can even make you seem confrontational. You'll usually get better results with a more informal arrangement, sitting on adjacent sides of a conference table.

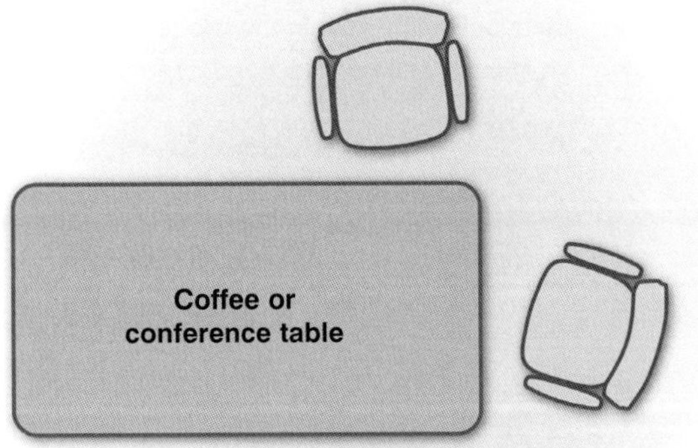

UNDERSTANDING BODY LANGUAGE

PROXIMITY

People are rarely at ease being physically close to strangers. The distance at which somebody feels comfortable varies according to factors such as:

- **Nationality:** Some cultures prefer closer contact than others
- **Background:** People from rural areas need more space
- **Status:** People keep further away from those with a higher perceived status
- **Gender:** Women are often comfortable being closer to other women than to men

People are usually only comfortable with family and close friends being nearer to them than 46cm, in their intimate zone. The personal zone (46cm-1.2m) is used for friendly gatherings, and the social zone (1.2m-3.6m) when dealing with strangers.

Positioning the chairs about 1.2m apart might help to strike an informal tone without invading somebody's personal space. You could also give the interviewee a choice of seats so they can choose one that matches their comfortable distance.

Source: zone distances from Body Language by Allan Pease

LOOKS/ APPEARANCE

The clothes that somebody wears to an interview convey the image they wish to project. Even where informal wear is common when carrying out the job, people often dress more formally for an interview.

Appearance will rarely tell you anything at all about whether somebody has the skills and experience to carry out a job, though, so don't let it distract you.

EXPRESSIONS OF EMOTION

The best way to judge the feelings and emotions of interviewees is to watch their faces.

Facial expressions convey emotions with much more accuracy than voice tone or even body posture.

So, when in doubt about how interviewees feel during an interview, watch their faces and trust your own judgement!

INTERPRETING BODY LANGUAGE

- **Don't mind read**. You can't be sure about the thought that triggered the body language response, or what the response means. Hand to face gestures can indicate deceit, but they might also indicate doubt, or even just that someone has an itch

- **Look for clusters of gestures**. Consider someone covering their mouth, for example – if they break eye contact suddenly, cover their mouth, and half-answer the question, it's different from somebody maintaining eye contact, covering their mouth, and then answering thoughtfully. In the first case, they might be lying, in the second they might just be buying thinking time

- **Context matters**. People cross their arms when they're cold. Some people might gesticulate or smile more than others. Look for changes in how that individual behaves. This can be hard to gauge in a short interview

- **Sudden changes matter**. If somebody changes their posture suddenly that can be a significant indicator

INTERPRETING BODY LANGUAGE

Don't leap to assumptions about what body language means, but use it to fine tune your questioning.

For example:

Interviewer   Tell me about your relationship with your previous manager.

Interviewee   (sits back suddenly and folds arms)
It was great. We worked well together.

Interviewer   What would you say was the most challenging
aspect of your working relationship?

You could also try moving on to a different topic, and then coming back to a more sensitive area once you've established rapport again.

USING YOUR OWN BODY LANGUAGE

Your own body language is a powerful communications tool. You can use it to make people feel comfortable, so they open up to you.

For example:
- Smile, genuinely. People can spot a fake smile easily
- Tilt your head slightly to show you're listening
- Maintain comfortable eye contact
- Maintain an open posture. Don't cross your arms or legs. The interviewee is likely to do the same, and feel less inclined to share information with you
- Respect the interviewee's personal space
- Dress appropriately. Overdressing can make candidates feel intimidated. Appearing too casual might be interpreted as a lack of interest in the interview process

MIRRORING BODY POSTURE

When you are with someone you like you unconsciously adapt your body posture to match theirs. You'll lean forward on the desk when they do, cross your legs as they do or put your elbow on the table as they do.

Good listeners intuitively 'mirror' a speaker's body posture, whether they are best friends or not, because they know it helps rapport.

As you start practising to become a better interviewer, why not do it consciously? It soon becomes second nature.

ECHOING TALKING SPEED

Good interviewers pace the speed of their speech to that of the interviewee. Someone who is excited about something will speak rapidly and animatedly.

If you respond with a similar 'excited speed', the interviewee is more likely to continue giving useful information. If she or he is being cautiously slow or hesitant in speech delivery, then an 'echo' of that caution in your questions and comments will show your respect, courtesy and understanding of that person's feelings.

If an interviewee is talking too fast for you to take notes, try asking your questions more slowly. They might mirror your talking speed and slow down.

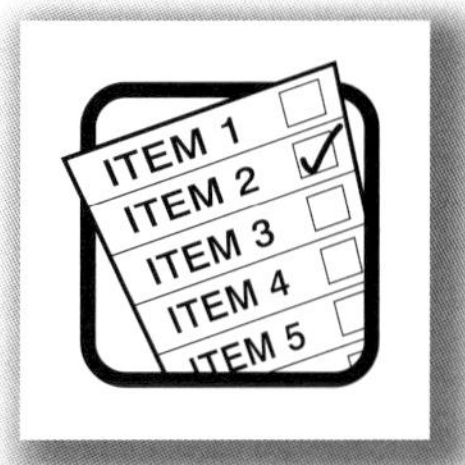

PREPARING FOR THE INTERVIEW

PREPARING FOR THE INTERVIEW

Good interview preparation is essential:

- It enables you to be sure you get the information you need from the candidate, because you can enter the room with an idea of what you need to know

- That takes the pressure off you as an interviewer, so you can more easily focus on listening to the candidate's replies

- Good preparation enables you to provide a consistent interview experience to all candidates, ensuring the process is fair

- It can also eliminate common barriers to successful communication

THE CANDIDATE'S INFORMATION

Whether you are interviewing internal or external candidates for a vacant position, you will need a written data sheet on each candidate before you begin the interviewing process.

There are three kinds of candidate data sheet:
1.   Standardised application form – external candidate.
2.   CV/ résumé – external candidate.
3.   Job history/ personal file – internal candidate.

Whichever you choose, ensure that you have consistent data on each candidate.

The information you have will provide valuable context to the candidate's answers during the interview.

CHECKING THE CANDIDATE'S INFORMATION

Everybody (including you) tries to look as good as possible on their CV/ résumé.

When preparing for the interview, note down any important questions you have on:

- Missing months/ years
- Seemingly incomplete or exaggerated educational achievements
- Seemingly over-stated job titles/ responsibilities

Don't let the CV dictate the agenda of the interview, though. Details of the candidate's **relevant** experience will come as you ask **your** questions.

Remember:

- The CV tells you what the **candidate** wants to tell you
- Your questions should find out what **you** need to know

THE JOB DESCRIPTION

An up-to-date **job description** is essential for a good selection interview. Otherwise, how can you give a true picture of the job? If you don't have one, there's a risk that some parts of the job which you discuss in the interview might later turn out not to be in the job, or tasks which are not mentioned come to light only when the candidate starts.

Without one, a new recruit might be **disappointed**, **frustrated**, **incompetent** or **scared** when they begin.

The job description also helps you to identify the skills and qualities you are looking for, which will be defined in the **job specification**.

THE JOB DESCRIPTION

A good job description covers at least five elements of the job:

1. Accountabilities/ responsibilities/ duties
The activities for which the position holder is responsible, including any deliverables.

2. Dimensions
The level or size of the responsibility (ie: sales, budget, people responsibility, functional reports, capital equipment).

3. Framework
Where does the job fit into the organisation?

4. Relationships
With whom does the position holder interact, both inside and outside the organisation? Who does the position holder report to?

5. Location
Including any travel requirements and home working.

THE JOB SPECIFICATION

Once you know what the job is (the job description), you have to decide what kind of person you need to do it.

A **job specification** sets out the minimum **person requirements** for the job. It includes the skills, experience and qualities that the person must have to perform the job successfully.

If you have not specified the kind of person you need, how can you judge whether any interviewee fits the bill?

THE JOB SPECIFICATION

To write the job specification, consider the skills, knowledge, behaviours and experience the person **must** have to be able to carry out the job.

Don't include things you might consider 'nice to have' or things that are unrelated to the ability to carry out the job.

Be as **specific** as possible. You might think you need a 'good team player', but that's too vague to be meaningful. You might need, for example:

- Someone who helps colleagues when they're overloaded
- Someone who inspires the team to work hard and meet deadlines
- Someone who shares sales leads with colleagues

Knowing the behaviour you need enables you to work out the right interview question to ask.

THE JOB SPECIFICATION

The specification might include things like:

- Certifications or professional qualifications
- Experience using particular technologies
- Written or spoken competency in foreign languages
- Experience delivering presentations
- Ability to meet tough deadlines
- Ability to come up with creative product ideas
- Track record in growing sales accounts
- Experience managing budgets for trade shows
- Health and safety knowledge
- Willingness to help others who are overloaded
- Commitment to exceptional customer service

QUANTIFYING THE JOB SPECIFICATION

Where possible, you should quantify the job specifications. Including measurable specifications in the job advert avoids underqualified candidates wasting their time, and also makes it easier for you to shortlist candidates for interview with confidence.

For example:

- Typing speed of at least 60 words per minute
- Has ACCA accountancy qualification
- Has a year's experience managing an international team
- Has managed budgets of £1m or more

Don't set barriers unnecessarily high because that will shrink the pool of candidates you can choose from. For example, if you're recruiting someone to manage a budget of £2m, you might decide this could be done by someone who has previously managed a budget of £1.5m. Similarly, don't assume everyone needs three years' experience to become a great salesperson.

PREPARING EVIDENCE QUESTIONS

To find out whether somebody fulfils the less quantifiable role requirements in the job specification, ask the candidate to tell you when they have demonstrated them in the past. That might be in a previous role, or could be through interests outside of work. Eg:

- Tell me about a time you delivered an important presentation
- Tell me about a recent time you used your French on the phone
- Describe a time when you had to meet a tough deadline
- Give me an example of when you came up with a new product idea
- Tell me about a time you grew sales within a customer account
- Give me an example of when you managed the budget for a trade show 

To ensure interviews are comparable (and the process is fair), you should have a standard list of initial questions you will ask every candidate. These questions will steer the interview, although you will ask different follow-up questions to drill down into the detail in each case. It might take **10 minutes** to get to the detail of each question, so don't have too many! Remember, you can invite promising candidates back for a further interview.

PREPARING ANSWERS

Candidates will have questions for you too, about the job and the company.

For example, they might want to know:

- Why has this position become vacant, or is being created?
- What opportunities are there to progress in the company?
- What are the short, medium and long term objectives of the role?
- Who are the people they would be working with?
- How is the company performing financially?
- What kind of culture does the company have?
- What hours do people usually work?
- What are the biggest challenges in this role?
- What are the biggest challenges working in this company?
- What kind of support is there for training and mentoring?

SHORTLISTING APPLICANTS

Shortlisting consists of choosing a relatively small number of candidates to interview from the total applications available. In many organisations this is the job of the human resources department.

Shortlisting involves comparing each application to the job specification and selecting those 'paper' candidates who seem to fit best.

NOTE: If the application contains insufficient data then ask for more or give the benefit of the doubt and shortlist for an interview.

SCHEDULING THE INTERVIEW

Contact candidates to agree mutually convenient times for their interviews. You might need to start early or finish late to minimise disruption to the interviewee's current job. Tell them how long you expect the interview to take (between 30 and 60 minutes is a good guide).

If appropriate, ask them to bring work samples with them, and warn them if you would like them to take any kind of test (such as a writing test) while they're with you.

PREPARING THE INTERVIEW ROOM

CHECKLIST

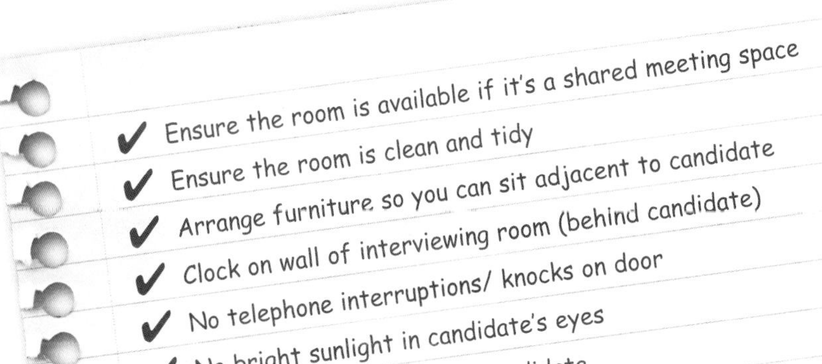

PREPARING THE INTERVIEW ROOM

Take with you:

- The interviewee's CV, résumé, application form or staff record
- Job description
- Job specification
- Preparatory notes and question list
- Notepad
- Business card
- Any company/ organisational literature

CONDUCTING THE INTERVIEW

MEETING THE CANDIDATE

GREETING

- Remember, the candidate is always nervous
- Be warm and friendly. Smile!
- Get up if you're seated
- Shake hands
- Use small talk about the journey, weather, building or parking to put the candidate at their ease
- Offer the candidate a drink (water, tea, coffee)

OPENING THE INTERVIEW

- Thank the candidate for coming to see you

- Introduce yourself, and your role in the company

- Explain the purpose of the interview is for you to learn about the candidate's skills and experience, and for the candidate to decide whether this is the right job for them

- Give the candidate a brief outline of the job you're recruiting for. It will help them to give you more relevant answers to your questions

- Warn the candidate that you'll be taking notes

OPENING THE INTERVIEW

EXAMPLE

Thank you for coming in today. My name is Bob Jones, and I manage the warehouse here. I've invited you to interview so I can learn more about your skills and experience, and so you can find out more about the job and see whether it's right for you. The role we're recruiting for is a team leader, who will supervise the ten people on the day shift. I've got some questions here, which will help me to find out more about your skills and past experience. To help me remember, I'll make notes while I listen to your answers. At the end of the interview, I'll set aside time for any further questions you have. OK? Let's begin!

THE INTERVIEW PROCESS

Ask any questions arising from the CV or application (see page 72)

Ask one of your standard questions (see page 79)

Listen to the candidate and take notes (see page 48)

Maintain eye contact as much as possible and comfortable (see page 59)

Try mirroring the candidate's posture and talking speed (see pages 67, 68)

Use reflective questions to encourage the candidate to keep talking (see page 27)

Clarify information with probing questions, challenge questions, blockbusting questions and framing questions (see pages 22-26)

Repeat with the next standard question until you've asked them all

Ask if the candidate has any questions for you and answer them (see page 80)

Close the interview (see page 103)

AN INTERVIEW EXAMPLE

The following pages contain an example of how an interview might run after the initial introductions, and how the interviewer can draw upon some of the different techniques you've learned about in this book.

Checking the candidate's information

CONDUCTING THE INTERVIEW

AN INTERVIEW EXAMPLE

Checking candidate meets quantifiable job specification requirement for 2 years' experience with the software

Interviewer 'OK, so tell me about your experience with XYZ software?'

Interviewee 'I've been using it for three years now. I use it all the time in my current role.'

First evidence question from the list of questions

Interviewer 'Excellent – we standardise on it. Tell me about a time you grew sales within a customer account.'

Interviewee 'I usually aim to get about 10% year on year growth from a customer account. That typically means looking at what we can upsell into them.'

AN INTERVIEW EXAMPLE

Keeping the interviewee on track

Interviewer 'That's great, but I'd really like to hear about a specific example.'

Interviewee 'I had a large pharmaceutical company as an account. They already had all of our software, but we noticed they weren't using any of our support services yet.'

Probing question: who

Interviewer 'When you say 'we', who else was involved in this?'

Interviewee 'The financial director. I asked her to confirm whether they had any service subscriptions when I realised there might be an opportunity there.'

AN INTERVIEW EXAMPLE

Reflective question

Interviewer 'And she would be the best person to know?'

Interviewee 'That's right. I was new to the account at the time, so I was still finding my feet.'

Probing question: when

Interviewer 'When was this?'

Interviewee 'About six months ago.'

AN INTERVIEW EXAMPLE

AN INTERVIEW EXAMPLE

Empathetic linking

Interviewer 'I can imagine! Tell me how you approached them?'

Interviewee 'I apologised and said that I was really sorry our software had let them down. I listened to all their concerns and I said I'd like to do what I could to help them.'

Backtrack frame

Interviewer 'What were your constraints at the time?'

Interviewee 'They weren't spending any money with us! I really did want to help, but we can't support products for free indefinitely.'

AN INTERVIEW EXAMPLE

Probing question: what

Interviewer 'So what did you do next?'

Interviewee 'I proposed a support agreement that would mean they never had a problem like that again.'

Blockbuster question

Interviewer 'Never?'

Interviewee 'Well, never that bad. We can get them up and running again in 12 hours under the support agreement.'

AN INTERVIEW EXAMPLE

Probing question

Interviewer 'So what was the outcome?'

Interviewee 'We negotiated for three months and they signed a deal worth £300,000 per year.'

Blockbuster question: verb

Interviewer 'How did you negotiate exactly?'

Interviewee 'I asked our legal team to draw up a contract, and we batted it back and forth between us and their procurement manager.'

AN INTERVIEW EXAMPLE

Probing question

Interviewer 'Did you give them a discount?'

Interviewee 'I try not to offer discounts if it can be avoided.'

Interviewer *Silence to prompt the candidate to reveal something they'd rather not.*

Interviewee 'On this occasion, I gave them a 20% discount. That was in exchange for a longer notice period than they initially wanted.'

AN INTERVIEW EXAMPLE

This sales approach is not easily repeatable, so the interviewer asks a hypothetical question to see whether the candidate knows how to sell to others too.

Interviewer 'It sounds like you really turned that account around. How would you sell services in somewhere that hadn't suffered a problem like this customer had?'

Interviewee 'I've prepared a presentation about what went wrong with this customer, and that's opened up discussions with two of our other existing clients about a possible service contract.'

AN INTERVIEW EXAMPLE

Devil's advocate challenge

Interviewer 'Some might argue it's a bad idea to showcase a product failure like that to your customers.'

Interviewee 'This particular problem was caused by the customer's team updating some software incorrectly, so it wasn't our fault. But it's the kind of thing that could happen anywhere, so our other customers recognise the risk.'

Next evidence question from the list

Interviewer 'Thank you. Next, I'd like to hear about a time you...'

HOW SUCCESSFUL WAS THE INTERVIEW?

In this example, the interviewer:

- Kept the candidate on track when they answered an evidence question as if it was a hypothetical question

- Used probing questions to find out exactly who was involved, and how much leadership the candidate had in this particular incident

- Probed to get a good understanding of the process and its outcome

- Used silence to press for information the candidate would rather not concede

- Used a hypothetical question to enable the candidate to elaborate on how they might sell in to other accounts

The interviewer has gathered solid evidence to show that the candidate is able to grow a sales account, one of the requirements in the job specification.

ANSWERING THE CANDIDATE'S QUESTIONS

Now it's your turn to answer the questions!

Plan enough time for candidates to ask you what they want to about the role and the company.

This is an important part of the interview: good candidates always have a choice, so you want to inspire them to want to work with you.

You need to sell the opportunity to the candidate, but you should be honest about any negative aspects of the role too. There will be fewer problems, and less risk of somebody leaving, if they enter the organisation with realistic expectations.

CLOSING THE INTERVIEW

At the end of the interview, thank the interviewee for coming and let them know the next steps in the recruitment process, including any follow-up interviews or tests that will take place.

Tell them when they should expect to hear, and how you will contact them.

EVALUATING CANDIDATES

After the interview, use your notes to evaluate the candidate:

- Check that they meet the requirements of the job specification
- Summarise the evidence that shows they meet these requirements
- Keep your notes to justify any hiring decision in the unlikely event that there is a claim of discrimination
- If you are interviewing lots of candidates, consider creating a decision matrix that enables you to easily compare candidates' capabilities in different areas, scoring them out of ten

EVALUATING CANDIDATES

MATRIX

Job specification	Candidates			
	1: Mason	2: Gilmour	3: Wright	4: Waters
Managed £1m+ budget	8	8	6	9
Experience managing global team	5	9	6	9
Experience growing sales	6	9	6	9
Experience selling to C-level				
Fluency in French				
Fluency in German				
TOTAL				

REFERENCE CHECKING

Never hire a candidate without checking references.

Some golden rules for reference checking:

- Always try to contact referees by **phone**, not in writing

- Pinpoint a possibly negative item from your interview with the candidate and ask the referee to comment. Repeat as necessary and listen to **how** the answer is given

- Finish by asking 'Would you re-hire this person if he/she came back to you for a job?' Be wary of any hesitation. Referees can **always** find a job for top performers

FOLLOW-UP

Always follow up on every interview by informing the candidate of the outcome of the interview.

- Thanks but no thanks (dead file)
- Not now but maybe later (active file)
- Still too early for a decision (pending)
- Next step (ie second interview)
- Contract on its way

Remember
The reputation of your organisation is closely bound to the way you treat ex-candidates.

About the Authors

Sean McManus

Sean McManus writes inspiring books about business and technology. He is co-author of The Customer Service Pocketbook. His other books include *Web Design in Easy Steps, iPad for the Older and Wiser, Microsoft Office for the Older and Wiser, Scratch Programming in Easy Steps*, and *Raspberry Pi For Dummies*. His magazine contributions have appeared in *Marketing Week, Customer Loyalty Today* and *Business 2.0* among others. Visit his website at www.sean.co.uk for bonus content and free chapters from his books.

John Townsend BA MA MCIPD

John has built a reputation as a leading trainer of trainers. He is founder of the highly-regarded Master Trainer Institute, a total learning facility located just outside Geneva which draws trainers and facilitators from around the world. He set up the institute after 30 years' experience in international consulting and human resources management positions in the UK, France, the United States and Switzerland – notably as a European Director of Executive development with GTE in Geneva where he had training responsibility for over 800 managers in 15 countries. During his long career as a trainer of trainers he has not only helped to spread unique Master Trainer Institute philosophy across the world via his conferences, seminars and bestselling training videos, but also written a number of widely translated management and professional guides.

Pocketbooks – *available in both paperback and digital formats*

360 Degree Feedback*
Absence Management
Appraisals
Assertiveness
Balance Sheet
Body Language
Business Planning
Career Transition
Coaching
Cognitive Behavioural Coaching
Communicator's
Competencies
Confidence
Creative Manager's
C.R.M.
Cross-cultural Business
Customer Service
Decision-making
Delegation
Developing People
Discipline & Grievance
Diversity*
Emotional Intelligence
Empowerment*
Energy and Well-being
Facilitator's
Feedback
Flexible Working*

Handling Complaints
Handling Resistance
Icebreakers
Impact & Presence
Improving Efficiency
Improving Profitability
Induction
Influencing
Interviewer's
I.T. Trainer's
Key Account Manager's
Leadership
Learner's
Management Models
Manager's
Managing Assessment Centres
Managing Budgets
Managing Cashflow
Managing Change
Managing Customer Service
Managing Difficult Participants
Managing Recruitment
Managing Upwards
Managing Your Appraisal
Marketing
Mediation
Meetings
Memory

Mentoring
Motivation
Negotiator's
Networking
NLP
Nurturing Innovation
Openers & Closers
People Manager's
Performance Management
Personal Success
Positive Mental Attitude
Presentations
Problem Behaviour
Project Management
Psychometric Testing
Resolving Conflict
Reward
Sales Excellence
Salesperson's*
Self-managed Development
Starting In Management
Storytelling
Strategy
Stress
Succeeding at Interviews
Sustainability
Tackling Difficult Conversations
Talent Management

Teambuilding Activities
Teamworking
Telephone Skills
Telesales*
Thinker's
Time Management
Trainer's
Training Evaluation
Training Needs Analysis
Transfer of Learning
Virtual Teams
Vocal Skills
Working Relationships
Workplace Politics
Writing Skills

** only available as an e-book*

Pocketfiles

Trainer's Blue Pocketfile of
Ready-to-use Activities

Trainer's Green Pocketfile of
Ready-to-use Activities

Trainer's Red Pocketfile of
Ready-to-use Activities

To order please visit us at **www.pocketbook.co.uk**

You may also find the *Body Language Pocketbook* of interest.

Your details

Name _______________________________

Position _______________________________

Company _______________________________

Address _______________________________

____

____

Telephone _______________________________

Fax _______________________________

E-mail _______________________________

VAT No. (EC companies) _______________________________

Your Order Ref _______________________________

Please send me:

No. copies

The Interviewer's ____________ Pocketbook [ ]

The ____________ Pocketbook [ ]

The ____________ Pocketbook [ ]

The ____________ Pocketbook [ ]

Order by Post
MANAGEMENT POCKETBOOKS LTD
LAUREL HOUSE, STATION APPROACH,
ALRESFORD, HAMPSHIRE SO24 9JH UK
Order by Phone, Fax or Internet
Telephone: +44 (0)1962 735573
Facsimile: +44 (0)1962 733637
Email: sales@pocketbook.co.uk
Web: www.pocketbook.co.uk

Customers in USA should contact:
Management Pocketbooks
2427 Bond Street, University Park, IL 60466
Telephone: 866 620 6944   Facsimile: 708 534 7803
Email: mp.orders@ware-pak.com
Web: www.managementpocketbooks.com